EXPLORERS

Sir Walter
Raleigh

Kristin Petrie

ABDO
Publishing Company

visit us at
www.abdopublishing.com

Published by ABDO Publishing Company, 4940 Viking Drive, Edina, Minnesota 55435.
Copyright © 2007 by Abdo Consulting Group, Inc. International copyrights reserved in all countries. No part of this book may be reproduced in any form without written permission from the publisher. The Checkerboard Library™ is a trademark and logo of ABDO Publishing Company.

Printed in the United States.

Cover Photos: Corbis
Interior Photos: Corbis pp. 7, 9, 11, 15, 23, 24, 25, 29; Getty Images pp. 5, 13; North Wind pp. 17, 19, 21, 28

Series Coordinator: Heidi M. Dahmes
Editors: Heidi M. Dahmes, Megan M. Gunderson
Art Direction & Cover Design: Neil Klinepier
Interior Design & Maps: Dave Bullen

Library of Congress Cataloging-in-Publication Data

Petrie, Kristin, 1970-
  Sir Walter Raleigh / Kristin Petrie.
    p. cm. -- (Explorers)
  Includes index.
  ISBN-10 1-59679-748-7
  ISBN-13 978-1-59679-748-2
  1. Raleigh, Walter, Sir, 1552?-1618--Juvenile literature. 2. Great Britain--Court and courtiers--Biography--Juvenile literature. 3. Explorers--Great Britain--Biography--Juvenile literature. I. Title. II. Series.

  DA86.22.R2P48 2006
  942.05'5'092--dc22

                                                                    2005017503

Contents

4

Sir Raleigh

Sir Walter Raleigh is one of the most colorful men in English history. Raleigh first appeared in records as a courageous soldier. He made a name for himself at battles in both France and Ireland.

Returning to England, Raleigh became a favorite of Queen Elizabeth I. He stayed in good standing with her for ten years. During that time, Raleigh received special privileges. And, the queen increased his **status** by knighting him.

Raleigh was a man of vision. He organized and **sponsored** expeditions to the New World. Without ever setting foot in North America, he established colonies there. And, he later became an explorer himself when he searched for the fabled **El Dorado** in South America.

Raleigh was also a writer. He published many works, including a poem called "The Lie" and a book titled *The History of the World*. Raleigh was a soldier, an explorer, a knight, and a poet.

1271
Polo left for Asia

1295
Polo returned to Italy

1254
Marco Polo born

1275
Polo met Kublai Khan

Sir Walter Raleigh lived an adventurous life both at home in England and abroad.

1460 or 1474
Juan Ponce de León born

1480
Ferdinand Magellan born

1324
Polo died

1475
Vasco Núñez de Balboa born

Early Life

Walter Raleigh was born in the **county** of Devon, England, around 1554. His father was also named Walter. His mother was Katherine. She was Walter's third wife. Walter had an older brother and an older sister. Because of his father's previous marriages, Walter also had many half brothers and half sisters.

Devon was a farming community. Walter's family lived in a farmhouse called Hayes Barton. It was near the English Channel and not far from the sea.

The Raleigh family was not wealthy. To make matters worse, Walter was not the firstborn son. This meant he would not inherit his father's home or land. So, Walter would need to earn a living another way.

At a young age, Walter heard tales of treasure in far-off lands. He heard stories of pirates, which excited him. And,

1500
Balboa joined expedition to South America

1493
Ponce de León joined expedition to New World

1502
Ponce de León became governor of Higüey

Would You?

**Would you be inspired by pirate stories?
Do you find them exciting or scary?**

Today, agriculture is still very important to the people of Devon.

his father participated in **privateering** expeditions with the famous Drake family. All of these things guided young Walter toward a life of adventure.

1508
Ponce de León's first expedition

1514
Ponce de León knighted by King Ferdinand II

1513
Ponce de León's second expedition, discovered Florida and the Gulf Stream; Balboa was the first European to sight the Pacific Ocean

Religious Wars

Little is known about Walter's life until he was a young adult. It is known that John Ford **tutored** Walter and his brother Carew. Historians also believe that the brothers attended the school of Ottery St. Mary.

During Walter's youth, there was much turmoil in England. **Protestants** and Catholics were frequently fighting for religious control. Walter's family contained many proud Protestants.

In 1558, Queen Elizabeth I came to power in England. Elizabeth had been raised a Protestant. She made the Church of England the country's main church. But this did not stop the conflicts.

In 1569, Walter traveled to France. There, he joined the Huguenots, or French Protestants, in their fight against Catholicism. The battles were horrible, and the Huguenots were defeated.

1520
Magellan discovered the Strait of Magellan

1554
Walter Raleigh born

1519
Magellan led expedition to Spice Islands; Balboa died

1521
Ponce de León's third expedition, died in Cuba; Magellan died

Despite the loss, Walter returned to England with much ambition and **valor**. Following in his family's example, Walter became a bold **Protestant**. He entered Oriel College in Oxford in 1572. Three years later, he was studying at Middle Temple law college in London.

Queen Elizabeth I ruled England from 1558 to 1603.

Royal Ambitions

With his education behind him, Raleigh was ready for his next adventure. On June 11, 1578, Raleigh's half brother Sir Humphrey Gilbert received a **patent** from the queen. This document allowed Gilbert to seek profitable lands overseas. The patent was good for six years.

An expedition was quickly organized. Raleigh was named captain of the *Falcon*, which was one of seven ships. The men faced many difficulties. In fact, arguments and bad weather prevented every ship but the *Falcon* from leaving. When Raleigh and his crew left England, they disappeared for six months. It is believed that they participated in acts of **piracy**.

In 1580, Raleigh's life changed again. He joined the English army and traveled to Ireland. As captain, Raleigh was in charge of 100 men. Together, they battled Irish **rebels**. Raleigh gained recognition at the siege of Smerwick.

1580
John Smith born

1585
Raleigh knighted by Queen Elizabeth I

1565
Henry Hudson born

1584–1589
Raleigh sponsored expeditions

Back in England, Raleigh entered Queen Elizabeth's **court**. Raleigh was charming, handsome, funny, and daring. He quickly impressed the queen. And by 1582, he was one of her favorites. Because of this, she gave him land in Ireland and permission to form colonies in North America. He also received special trade privileges.

Some claim Raleigh won Queen Elizabeth's favor while she was out walking. They say Raleigh placed his cloak over a puddle so the queen would not muddy her shoes.

Sponsorships

Since Raleigh's youth, men of courage and adventure had surrounded him. He was eager to have exciting adventures, too. He had gained glory and respect in Ireland. Now, it was time for bigger experiences.

Unfortunately for Raleigh, the queen liked to keep her favorites nearby. This meant he had to stay in England. So, he participated in adventures from his London home called Durham House.

In 1583, Gilbert was planning an expedition to establish a colony in North America. Raleigh could not go along. So, he enthusiastically contributed money and a ship. If Gilbert discovered new land, Raleigh would receive a large plot in return.

On June 11, Gilbert set sail on his **flagship**, the *Bark Raleigh*. He was never seen again. Raleigh asked to take over Gilbert's **patent**. Queen Elizabeth agreed and gave him a six-year patent. But, she still kept him close by.

1595
Raleigh led first expedition

1588
Raleigh helped defeat the Spanish Armada

1606
Smith joined expedition to North America

Would You?

Would you enjoy just planning expeditions? Or, do you think you would like to participate in the adventures as well?

Sir Humphrey Gilbert

In April 1584, Raleigh sent out an expedition to the New World. The small **fleet** sailed across the Atlantic Ocean and the Caribbean Sea. After the ships reached the West Indies, they turned north to follow the North American coast.

The crew finally arrived at the Outer Banks. This island chain is part of today's North Carolina. Led by Captains Philip Amadas and Arthur Barlowe, the crew explored Roanoke Island. In July, the men walked onto North Carolina's mainland. They claimed the region for England.

In September, the crew returned to England. They brought with them two natives named Manteo and Wanchese. The crew also had samples of tobacco and potatoes.

The crew told amazing stories of their adventures. This quickly led to plans for another expedition. Raleigh was excited about the new land. He decided to name it Virginia.

Queen Elizabeth rewarded Raleigh for his role in claiming part of North America. She knighted him on January 6, 1585. Two years later, the queen named Raleigh captain of her guard. This was another honorable position.

1607
Hudson's first expedition

1609
Hudson's third expedition

1608
Hudson's second expedition

Raleigh is North Carolina's capital city. It is named for Sir Walter Raleigh.

1614
Smith led expedition to North America, charted and named New England

1610–1611
Hudson's last expedition, he died

1616
Raleigh's second expedition

By April 1585, another small **fleet** was prepared to sail to Virginia. Once again, Raleigh funded the expedition but remained in England. Sir Richard Grenville took Raleigh's place as leader.

On April 9, about 600 sailors, soldiers, and settlers left Plymouth, England. On July 3, they reached Roanoke Island. The voyage had been difficult, and a supply ship had wrecked.

Grenville soon returned to England for more supplies. While awaiting Grenville's return, the remaining settlers became discouraged. Their food supplies were running low, and many feared the natives.

In June 1586, Sir Francis Drake arrived at Roanoke. The colonists jumped at the chance to return to England with him. Despite the difficulties they had experienced, the colonists told Raleigh that the vast land held many possibilities.

1618
Raleigh died

1637
Jacques Marquette born

1645
Louis Jolliet born

1631
Smith died

1643
René-Robert Cavelier de La Salle born

Would you have abandoned the colony? What do you think Drake thought of Roanoke Island?

Grenville returned to Roanoke with supplies two weeks after the settlers had departed with Drake.

Lost Colony

Raleigh immediately began planning the next expedition to colonize Virginia. This time, artist and explorer John White was appointed leader. His group consisted of 14 families and 78 men.

Raleigh chose a promising new site for the colony. The previous expedition had discovered the Chesapeake Bay north of Roanoke. The bay was deep enough for large ships. And, some colonists had told Raleigh that the best planting would be in this area.

The voyagers set sail on May 8, 1587. But the **fleet**'s pilot, Simon Fernandez, did not follow Raleigh's plan. Fernandez was more interested in **privateering** than in settling new lands. So, he abandoned the colonists at Roanoke.

The settlers did their best to survive in the colony. But, they had little food and no way of getting more. So on August 27, 1587, White sailed back to England for supplies. Unfortunately, war between England and Spain kept him from returning until 1590.

1669
La Salle explored Ohio region

1666
La Salle sailed to Canada

1673
Marquette and Jolliet explored the Mississippi River

On August 18, 1587, the first English child was born in North America. Her name was Virginia Dare. What happened to the Roanoke settlers, including Dare, remains a mystery.

By the time White returned to Roanoke, there was no sign of the settlers. White found only the word "Croatoan" carved into a tree. Natives used this word for present-day Hatteras Island. So, White thought the colonists had moved. But, bad weather kept him from further explorations. Today, the settlement is remembered as the "lost colony."

Spanish Armada

In 1588, Raleigh had joined the fight against the Spanish **Armada**. He **donated** his ship the *Ark Raleigh* to the English naval forces.

Once again, Raleigh participated from shore. He was in charge of land defenses. Raleigh's men watched as the Spanish warships approached England. Under Raleigh's fearless leadership, the English troops were successful. Spanish troops failed to invade the coast. The armada eventually fell to English war **tactics** and bad weather.

By the early 1590s, Raleigh was at the height of his career. His successes in battle had earned him respect. And he was on the edge of adventure, seeking opportunities in North America. He was also wealthy. But most important, Raleigh remained one of Queen Elizabeth's favorites.

1675
Marquette died

1682
La Salle's second Mississippi River expedition

1679
La Salle's first Mississippi River expedition

English ships attacking the Spanish Armada

    Raleigh had also gained recognition as a poet. Among his many works is the poem titled "The Book of the Ocean to Cynthia." He also helped English poet Edmund Spenser publish his poem *The Faerie Queene*.

1687
La Salle died

1684
La Salle's third Mississippi River expedition

1700
Jolliet died

The Fall

Raleigh could not hold the queen's favor forever. In 1592, the queen questioned Raleigh's loyalty. Four years earlier, Raleigh had secretly married Elizabeth Throckmorton, one of the queen's attendants. That secret was revealed when Elizabeth gave birth to a son, who did not survive.

Queen Elizabeth was furious. As punishment, she locked both Walter and Elizabeth in the Tower of London. During his imprisonment, Raleigh wrote dramatic poems. He reflected on the many years he had held the queen's affections. And, he wrote about his fears of losing the **status** and the respect he had earned.

While the knight slowly lost all hope, one of his earlier endeavors paid off. Before his imprisonment, Raleigh had sent out **privateering** ships. Raleigh's men seized a treasure ship called the *Madre de Dios*. It was loaded with spices, pearls, silver, and gold.

1770
William Clark born

1786
Sacagawea born

1774
Meriwether Lewis born

1800
Sacagawea captured

The goods aboard the *Madre de Dios* were England's most valuable prize yet! The profits were divided between those who had funded the feat. However, the queen made sure that Raleigh received very little.

In Raleigh's time, the Tower of London served as both a prison and an execution site. Today, the tower is a historic landmark.

ENTRY TO THE TRAITORS' GATE

El Dorado

Raleigh was freed from the Tower of London in 1592. In 1593, Walter and Elizabeth had a second son, Walter. A third son, Carew, was born a few years later.

Out of the queen's favor, Raleigh needed a new mission. He could now experience adventure firsthand! So in 1595, Raleigh set sail for South America. He planned to search for the riches of the fabled kingdom of **El Dorado**.

Raleigh and his men sailed to present-day Venezuela and ventured inland. Raleigh surprised everyone with his respect for the natives. With their help, the expedition reached the Orinoco River. There, tribes warned the explorers about the huge army that protected El Dorado.

Raleigh wrote detailed accounts of everything he saw and heard. He noted

Raleigh and his son Walter who was also called Wat

1804
Lewis and Clark began exploring the Pacific Northwest

1806
Lewis and Clark returned to Missouri

1805
Sacagawea joined the Lewis and Clark expedition

Upon his return to England, Raleigh could not find anyone to support another expedition to El Dorado.

fertile land and rivers full of fish. His men also found stones that looked like sapphires. But, the natives continued to warn them of the dangers near **El Dorado**. Raleigh planned to return with a large English army.

Back in England, Raleigh romanticized his findings in a book titled *The Discoverie of Guiana*. He hoped the promise of rich new lands would win back Queen Elizabeth's favor. But, she refused to support a return expedition.

1812
Sacagawea died

1856
Robert Edwin Peary born

1809
Lewis died

1838
Clark died

1881
Peary entered the U.S. Navy

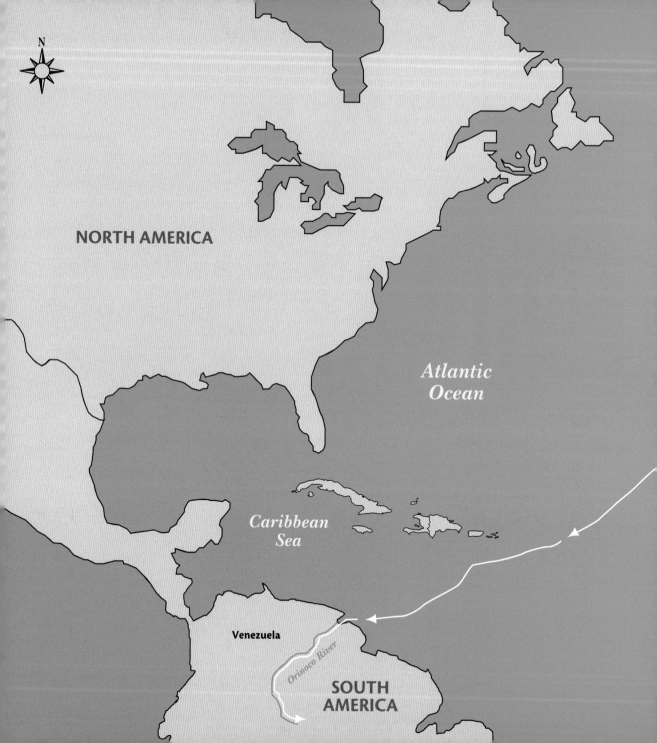

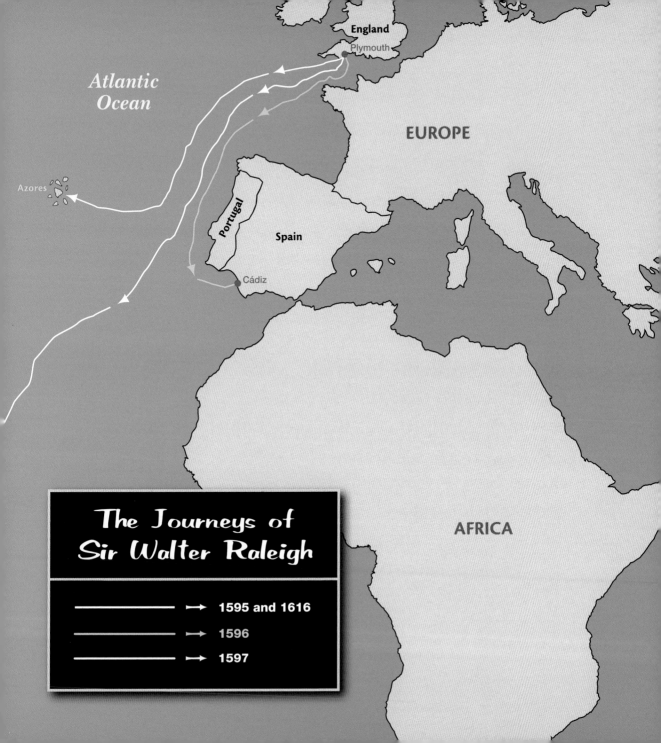

Atlantic
Ocean

EUROPE

Azores

Portugal

Spain

Cádiz

England
Plymouth

AFRICA

The Journeys of
Sir Walter Raleigh

1595 and 1616

1596

1597

Final Journeys

In 1596, Raleigh joined English nobleman Robert Devereux on a journey to Cádiz, Spain. The next year, Raleigh sailed with Devereux to the Azores, islands off Portugal's coast. Raleigh's efforts finally won back the queen's favor.

Queen Elizabeth died in 1603. Her replacement, King James I, did not trust Raleigh. He charged Raleigh with treason and locked him in the Tower of London. Raleigh spent the next 13 years in the tower. During that time, he devoted himself to writing. He wrote a book titled *The History of the World.*

The execution of Raleigh

1893
Peary's first expedition

1905
Peary's second expedition

Raleigh was released in 1616 to lead another expedition to South America. The king ordered Raleigh not to invade Spanish territory. But, Raleigh's crew disobeyed this command. Upon his return, Raleigh was sentenced to death. He was executed in London on October 29, 1618.

Sir Walter Raleigh left a colorful legacy. He was successful in battle, fighting fiercely for his faith and his country. He was both an **entrepreneur** and an explorer. He will be remembered throughout history for his contributions to the expansion of human knowledge.

You can view this statue of Raleigh at the Old Royal Naval College at Greenwich in London, England.

1909
Peary's third expedition, reached the North Pole

1920
Peary died

SIR
WALTER
RALEIGH

1552
1618

Glossary

armada - a group of warships.

county - a territorial division of England and Wales separated for administrative, judicial, and political purposes.

court - of or having to do with the residence, the advisers, or the assemblies of a ruler.

donate - to give.

El Dorado - a city or a country that explorers in the 1500s believed held fabulous riches and was located in South America.

entrepreneur - one who organizes, manages, and accepts the risks of a business or an enterprise.

flagship - the ship that carries the officer in command of a fleet or squadron and displays his flag.

fleet - a group of ships under one command.

patent - an official document giving a person the right or privilege to perform an act or a duty.

piracy - robbery on an open sea or ocean.

privateer - an armed private ship licensed to attack enemy ships.

Protestant - a Christian who does not belong to the Catholic Church.

rebel - to disobey an authority or the government. One who participates in acts of disobedience or armed resistance is a rebel.

sponsor - a person or a group of people who support someone, often financially.

status - a position or rank in a social or professional standing.

tactic - a method or a device used to achieve a goal.
tutor - to teach a student privately. The teacher is also called a tutor.
valor - great bravery.

Azores - uh-ZOHRZ
Cádiz - KAH-theeth
entrepreneur - ahn-truh-pruh-NUHR
Huguenot - HYOO-guh-naht
Roanoke - ROH-uh-nohk
Robert Devereux - RAHB-uhrt DEHV-uh-roo

To learn more about Sir Walter Raleigh, visit ABDO Publishing Company on the World Wide Web at **www.abdopublishing.com**. Web sites about Raleigh are featured on our Book Links page. These links are routinely monitored and updated to provide the most current information available.

Index